ELEPHANTS
Gentle Land Giants

by Isidro Sánchez
Illustrated by Gabriel Casadevall and Ali Garousi

Gareth Stevens Publishing
A WORLD ALMANAC EDUCATION GROUP COMPANY

Please visit our web site at: www.garethstevens.com
For a free color catalog describing Gareth Stevens Publishing's
list of high-quality books and multimedia programs,
call 1-800-542-2595 or fax your request to (414) 332-3567.

The editor would like to extend special thanks to Jan W. Rafert, Curator of Primates and Small Mammals, Milwaukee County Zoo, Milwaukee, Wisconsin, for his kind and professional help with the information in this book.

Library of Congress Cataloging-in-Publication Data

Sánchez, Isidro.
   [Elefante. English]
   Elephants: gentle land giants / by Isidro Sánchez; illustrated by Gabriel Casadevall and Ali Garousi.
      p. cm. – (Secrets of the animal world)
   Includes bibliographical references and index.
   Summary: Describes the physical characteristics and habits of elephants, including diet, elephant enemies and ancestors, and life in a herd.
   ISBN 0-8368-1635-8 (lib. bdg.)
   1. Elephants–Juvenile literature. [1. Elephants.] I. Casadevall, Gabriel, ill. II. Garousi, Ali, ill. III. Title. IV. Series.
QL737.P98S2513 1997
599.67–dc21   97-8484

This North American edition first published in 1997 by
Gareth Stevens Publishing
A World Almanac Education Group Company
330 West Olive Street, Suite 100
Milwaukee, Wisconsin 53212 USA

This U.S. edition © 1997 by Gareth Stevens, Inc. Created with original © 1993 Ediciones Este, S.A., Barcelona, Spain. Additional end matter © 1997 by Gareth Stevens, Inc.

Series editor: Patricia Lantier-Sampon
Editorial assistants: Diane Laska, Rita Reitci

Printed in the United States of America

2 3 4 5 6 7 8 9 06 05 04 03 02

CONTENTS

THE LARGEST LAND ANIMAL

The elephant's habitat

The elephant belongs to the scientific order Proboscidea, which has two species: African elephants and Asian elephants.

African elephants live in savannas, forests, areas near riverbanks, and in some jungles.

Asian elephants inhabit dense jungles, rain forests, and fertile areas of Asia, especially in India.

About 450,000 African elephants and 50,000 Asian elephants inhabit Earth today.

Elephants live in certain regions of Asia and Africa.

Two handlers help their elephants bathe. Domesticated Asian elephants help humans work.

What is a mammal?

Elephants are mammals. Mammals differ from other animals in the way they develop and give birth to their offspring.

Female birds, amphibians, reptiles, and fish lay eggs. Babies develop inside the eggs until they hatch. This is known as oviparous reproduction.

Some fish species also lay eggs that remain in the mother's body. Babies develop inside the eggs and are born totally formed. This is known as ovoviviparous reproduction.

Almost all female mammals are viviparous animals. Their young develop inside the mother's body in a muscular, baglike organ called the uterus. At birth, the babies resemble the adults, and suckle their mother's milk.

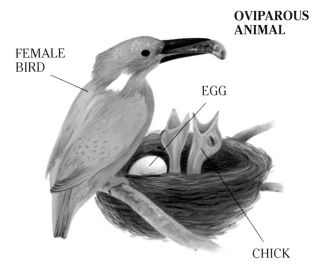

OVIPAROUS ANIMAL

FEMALE BIRD

EGG

CHICK

OVOVIVIPAROUS ANIMAL

FEMALE SHARK

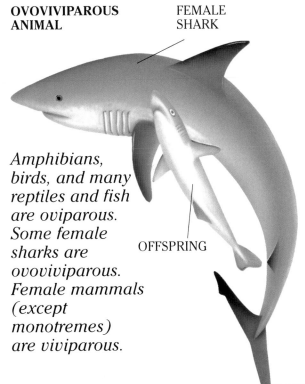

Amphibians, birds, and many reptiles and fish are oviparous. Some female sharks are ovoviviparous. Female mammals (except monotremes) are viviparous.

OFFSPRING

VIVIPAROUS ANIMAL

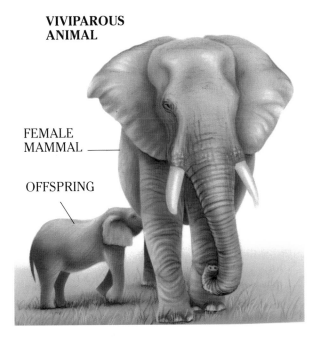

FEMALE MAMMAL

OFFSPRING

Different but the same

The only two elephant species in the world — African elephants and Asian elephants — are quite different. African elephants are larger, making them easy to identify when next to Asians.

African elephants measure up to 26 feet (8 meters) in length, including the trunk, and 13 feet (4 m) in height. African elephants can also weigh over 13,230 pounds (6,000 kilograms).

African elephants have huge ears, while Asian species have much smaller ones. African elephant tusks are longer than the tusks of the Asian elephants.

These drawings illustrate the differences between Asian and African elephants.

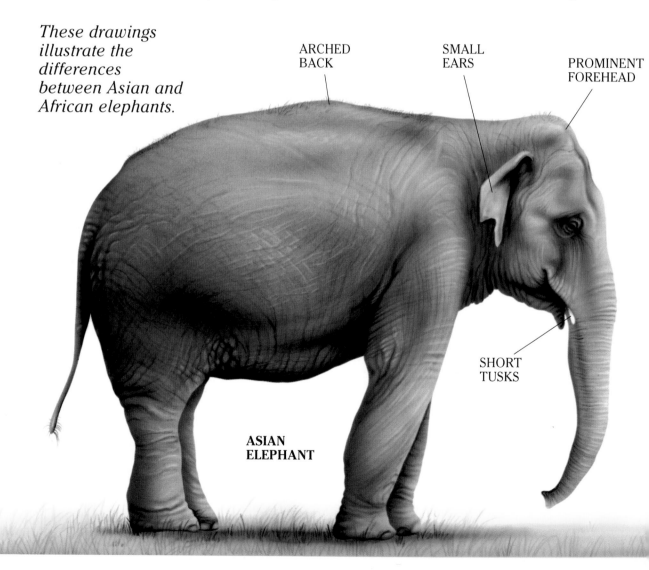

ARCHED BACK

SMALL EARS

PROMINENT FOREHEAD

SHORT TUSKS

ASIAN ELEPHANT

African elephant trunks have two lobes at the end, while Asian elephants have only one. African elephants also have a rounded forehead and a slightly sunken back, while Asian elephants have a more prominent forehead and a back that arches upward slightly.

Despite their tough and heavy feet, elephants practically walk on tiptoe. A thick cushion of fat protects their toes and supports the sole and heel of the foot.

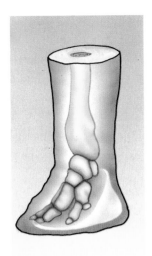

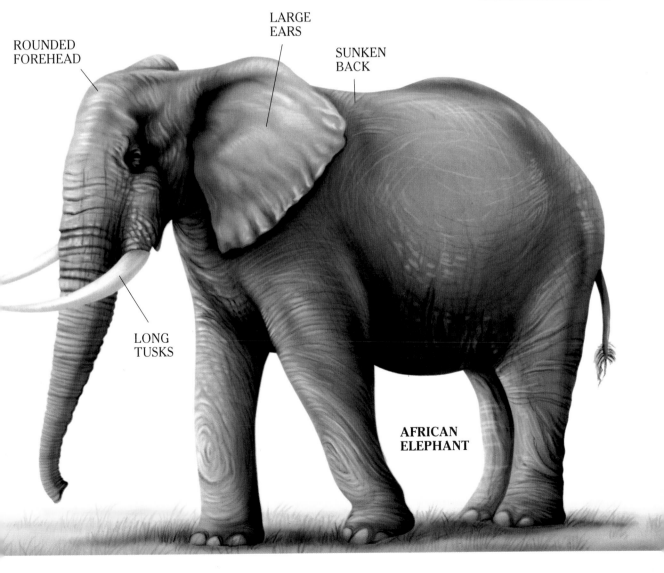

ROUNDED
FOREHEAD

LARGE
EARS

SUNKEN
BACK

LONG
TUSKS

**AFRICAN
ELEPHANT**

INSIDE THE ELEPHANT

The elephant body's length and height give it balance and strength. This enables the enormous animal to stand upright in spite of its incredible weight. Thick, broad feet help the elephant maintain its balance. The elephant's huge body can move quickly. An attacking or escaping elephant can run up to 25 miles (40 kilometers) an hour.

THICK SKIN
Elephant skin can be 1.5 inches (4 cm) thick. To keep its skin free of insects, the animal wallows in mud and sprays water over itself with its trunk.

SCAPULA

SPINAL COLUMN

STOMACH

KIDNEY

HIP

BLADDER

ELEPHANT FOOD
Elephants are herbivores. They eat all types of plants — grass, leaves, small branches, roots, bark, and fruit. The Asian elephant also eats bamboo.

FEMUR

INTESTINES

LIVER

ULNA

ELEPHANT TRACKS
The elephant's feet are wide. The fat layer protecting the toes acts like an elastic cushion. It is difficult to follow an elephant's tracks. The broad, cushioned feet leave only a faint imprint because the animal's weight is so evenly distributed.

TIBIA

CUSHION OF FAT

EATING HABITS
The elephant tears bark from trees with its tusks. It uses its trunk to grasp branches and fruit, and to place food in its mouth, which it chews with enormous teeth.

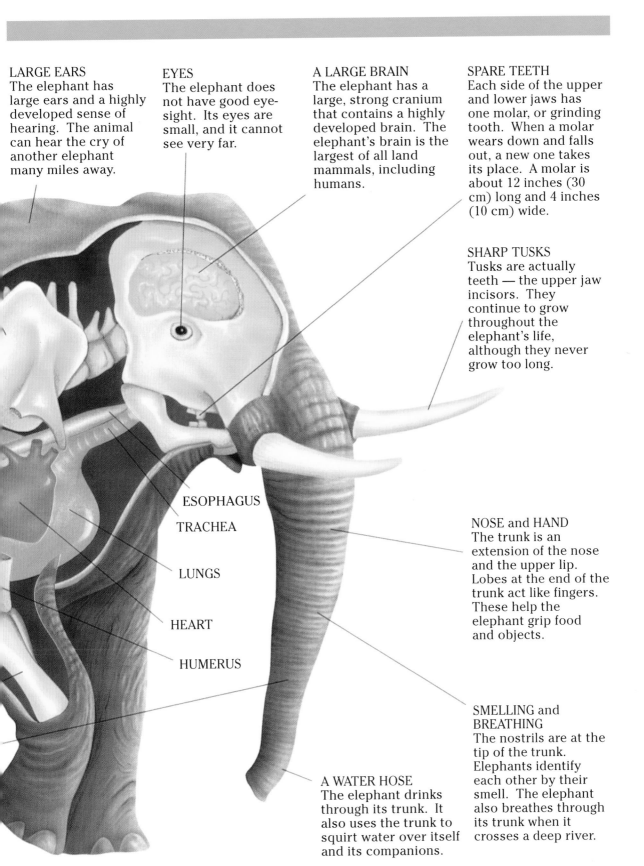

LARGE EARS
The elephant has large ears and a highly developed sense of hearing. The animal can hear the cry of another elephant many miles away.

EYES
The elephant does not have good eyesight. Its eyes are small, and it cannot see very far.

A LARGE BRAIN
The elephant has a large, strong cranium that contains a highly developed brain. The elephant's brain is the largest of all land mammals, including humans.

SPARE TEETH
Each side of the upper and lower jaws has one molar, or grinding tooth. When a molar wears down and falls out, a new one takes its place. A molar is about 12 inches (30 cm) long and 4 inches (10 cm) wide.

SHARP TUSKS
Tusks are actually teeth — the upper jaw incisors. They continue to grow throughout the elephant's life, although they never grow too long.

ESOPHAGUS

TRACHEA

LUNGS

HEART

HUMERUS

NOSE and HAND
The trunk is an extension of the nose and the upper lip. Lobes at the end of the trunk act like fingers. These help the elephant grip food and objects.

SMELLING and BREATHING
The nostrils are at the tip of the trunk. Elephants identify each other by their smell. The elephant also breathes through its trunk when it crosses a deep river.

A WATER HOSE
The elephant drinks through its trunk. It also uses the trunk to squirt water over itself and its companions.

BIRTH OF AN ELEPHANT

Searching for a mate

At certain times of the year, most male and female animals search for a mate. During this time, the animal is "in heat." The female elephant, or cow, is ready to mate once a year.

The mating period for cows lasts only a few days. Males, or bulls, either live alone or in small groups outside of the herds. They must travel long distances to be near the females at mating time. Males fight among themselves to prove their strength. The larger elephants usually win.

The mating period usually takes place during the rainy season, when there is more food and water available.

Adult male elephants usually live alone. But during the mating period, they gather in small groups and search for female herds.

that elephants and egrets help each other?

Different animal species often join together in unusual associations, known as symbiosis. In some of these relationships, such as the one between the elephant and the cattle egret, both animals benefit.

The egret usually lives in creeks, marshes, and other swampy areas. It feeds on larvae and small fishes. The cattle egret, however, lives close to elephant herds. It flies from one elephant to another to feed on the insects that accumulate on the animal's back. In this way, the elephant's back becomes free of insects, and the egret gets easy prey from the elephant.

A long pregnancy

Like all mammals, elephants develop their young as a result of sexual reproduction.

A male elephant places its spermatozoid, or reproductive cell, inside a female's body. There it enters, or fertilizes, a female reproductive cell, or ovum. Inside a muscular, baglike structure called the uterus, the fertilized ovum grows into a fetus, which keeps developing until it is ready to be born. The placenta, a special blood-rich organ, grows up against the inside of the uterus. The placenta passes food and oxygen from the mother through the umbilical cord to the fetus. It also takes away the baby's wastes. The mother carries the growing baby for about twenty-two months — nearly two years.

The female elephant is a viviparous animal, like all mammals (except the monotremes). The fetus develops inside the uterus of the mother.

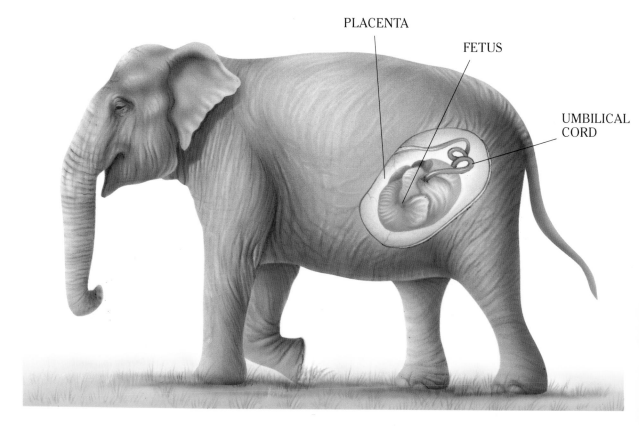

PLACENTA

FETUS

UMBILICAL CORD

A really big baby!

As the time approaches, the mother leaves the herd with two or three other cows and looks for a quiet place to give birth. The females that accompany the pregnant elephant remain at its side throughout the birth and help the newborn calf stand.

The calf's body is covered with long hairs. It sheds these hairs at the end of its first year, and its skin is tough and smooth.

The newborn elephant is one of the largest babies in the world. It measures 35 inches (90 cm) high and weighs about 265 pounds (120 kg).

Two or three cows of the herd usually accompany the pregnant elephant during birth.

At birth, the baby elephant is hairy and already has several milk teeth. But it is barely able to stand up.

The first year of life

Baby elephants, or calves, are well cared for. Soon after birth, the young elephant can stand up on its own, although it is too weak to walk. One of the calf's first actions is to feel its mother's body with its tiny trunk until it finds milk.

The calf suckles milk from its mother right after birth. For the first few months, it feeds only on its mother's milk.

The calf can keep up with the herd only a few days after birth.

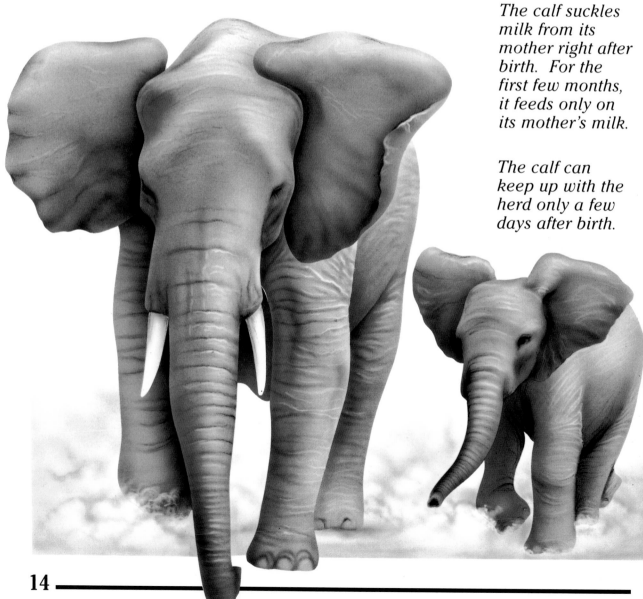

The baby elephant drinks its mother's milk by sucking the milk through its mouth. It feeds this way because it has not yet learned how to use its trunk.

A few days later, the baby's weak legs are strong enough for it to walk. At about six months, it begins to walk a little distance away from its mother. The mother and other members of the herd keep close watch on its movements.

The calf suckles until it is two years old, but at six months it also starts to take grass from its mother's mouth.

Baby elephants love to play. They invent invisible enemies or try to climb on the back of older brothers or cows as they sleep.

The cows of a herd never leave their young unattended, especially during the first few months.

The calf is very playful, particularly during its first year of life.

The young elephant

By the end of its first year of life, the calf has learned which plants are edible and how to pick grass to feed itself.

Before it reaches its second birthday, the calf will know how to get food during the dry season, when grass is scarce. It learns to use its tusks to tear bark from trees and dig roots from the ground. It takes longer for the calf to learn how to suck water into its trunk.

Female elephants look after their young longer than any other animal. A calf lives with its mother for about ten years.

This calf uses its trunk to pick leaves and put them in its mouth.

The young elephant tears bark from trees with its tusks.

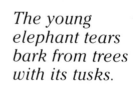

Elephants take more baths than any other animal. Young elephants love to play in the water.

that there are no such things as elephant graveyards?

Many people believe there are elephant graveyards. Legends tell how all the elephants of a certain region traveled to a cemetery to die when they got old.

Hundreds of adventurers have searched for these cemeteries, hoping to find ivory. Although it is true that many skeletons have been discovered close together, this does not necessarily mean that the elephants went there to die. Perhaps the skeletons were the result of an entire herd dying at the same time. Or the elephants may have died of thirst near a dried-up watering hole.

HOW ELEPHANTS LIVE

Life in the herd

Female elephants are social. They live in groups called herds. They form families of offspring, aunts, and cousins and work together to protect each other from enemies and other dangers.

Family life in the herd is ruled by the oldest cow, called the matriarch. This matriarch guides the herd because of her experience. She knows the dangers the group will confront and how to avoid them.

Adult bulls are less social. They usually live alone. If a group of bulls does form a herd, each still acts separately. They do not work together to find food or defend one another.

An elephant herd drinks in a river. Each elephant sucks water up into its trunk and then squirts it into its mouth.

An elephant herd (1) is formed by a cow and its young. A family group within a herd is made up of a mother and its youngest offspring (2), together with older offspring (3). A single herd can consist of several families (4).

The elephant's enemies

Adult elephants are so big and strong they have few enemies. Young elephants, however, can be attacked by lions and hyenas in Africa, or by tigers in Asia. Members of a herd defend each other. If one of them is wounded, the others go to its aid, even though they risk their own safety. An angry elephant is very dangerous. To scare away an enemy, an elephant extends its ears to appear bigger and makes loud, trumpeting noises. But in attacking, an elephant gives no warning. It just tucks up its trunk and charges.

The lion preys on young elephants that have strayed from the herd.

An attacking elephant is an awesome and frightening spectacle as it shakes the ground during its charge.

4

1

Elephants and humans

Humans are the only true enemy of the elephant. Because ivory is worth a great deal of money, ivory poachers have hunted the elephant for many years.

Most African elephants live in national parks, where it is against the law to hunt them.

Asian elephants have been domesticated for thousands of years. In the past, during times of war, they were trained to carry heavy equipment. Today, Asian elephants in India and other countries carry logs, transport people, and take part in ceremonial processions.

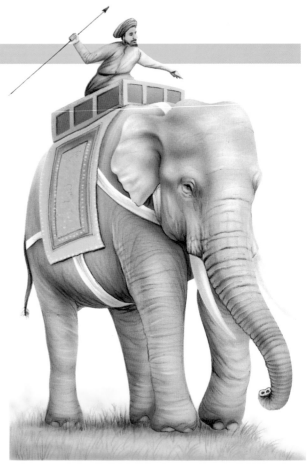

At one time, elephants carried humans and heavy weapons to war.

Today, elephants in India are used to carry logs.

that some elephants play soccer?

In some Asian countries, elephants are part of daily life. They are domesticated animals that work at many agricultural tasks. For this reason, one day each year celebrates the elephant.

During the Day of the Elephant, the animals do not work. The villagers decorate the animals and allow them to run in races or even play soccer! The elephants play with riders that steer the animals to hit the ball or tackle with their trunk. Only cows can play, since they do not have tusks.

GIANTS OF THE PAST

Moeritherium was one of the oldest ancestors of the elephant.

Enormous mastodon

The two existing species of elephant — the African and Asian elephants — are the only survivors of a wide variety of giants that inhabited Earth millions of years ago.

The elephant's first ancestor, Moeritherium, was similar in size and appearance to the tapir. It lived 40 million years ago.

The elephant's most direct ancestors were the gigantic mastodons. The mastodons had a trunk and big tusks over 10 feet (3 m) long. They were covered with hair and could stand the terrible cold of prehistoric times.

The impressive mastodon was the elephant's ancestor. It lived more than 40 million years ago.

Mammoth of the ice

The mammoth was another elephant ancestor. It lived during the prehistoric period known as the Quaternary. Scientists have discovered — preserved in ice — the skin and fur of this gigantic ancestor of the elephant.

The mammoth grew up to 16 feet (5 m) in height, and its tusks extended 13 feet (4 m) in length. Long black and red hairs protected it from the cold. It also had a coat of thick, shorter hairs and a layer of fat 3 inches (8 cm) thick.

About 10,000 years ago, prehistoric humans began hunting the mammoth for food and clothing.

The mammoth lived during the Ice Age. Its thick hair protected it from the cold.

Humans hunted the mammoth by digging a hole in the ground. When the animal fell in, they killed it by throwing rocks and spears.

APPENDIX TO

SECRETS
OF THE
ANIMAL WORLD

ELEPHANTS
Gentle Land Giants

ELEPHANT SECRETS

A heavy animal. The African elephant can weigh up to 13,230 pounds (6,000 kg), about as much as 100 people!

▼ Taking turns. At a water hole, the herd's leader always drinks first, then the other cows. The younger elephants and the calves drink last.

▲ Huge fans. Elephants use their huge ears, up to 5 feet (1.5 m) high and 1.6 feet (0.5 m) wide, to fan themselves and to scare enemies.

▲ Trumpets ahoy! Elephants trumpet when angry or scared, or to communicate with others.

▼ **Multipurpose trunk.** The elephant uses its trunk to breathe, smell, eat, and drink. Young elephants use it to hold on to their mother's tail so they don't get lost. Elephants also use the trunk as a "hand-shake" to help them recognize each other. One elephant inserts its trunk into the mouth of the other. This is its way of saying "hello."

1. What species of elephants exist today?
   a) The European and American.
   b) The African and the Asian.
   c) Pygmy, tropical, and desert.

2. To what group of animals do the elephants belong?
   a) Reptiles.
   b) Amphibians.
   c) Mammals.

3. What is the elephant's method of reproduction?
   a) Oviparous.
   b) Viviparous.
   c) Ovoviviparous.

4. How does the baby elephant suckle from its mother?
   a) With its trunk.
   b) With its mouth.

5. How long does a young elephant stay with its mother?
   a) Until it is ten to twelve years old.
   b) Until it is one year old.
   c) Until it is six years old.

6. How do male elephants live?
   a) With females in a herd.
   b) With their offspring, until the young reach six years of age.
   c) They live alone or in small groups.

The answers to ELEPHANT SECRETS questions are on page 32.

GLOSSARY

agriculture: the practice of raising crops and livestock.

ancestors: previous generations of a family or species.

confront: to face or meet aggressively, as in an argument or fight.

domesticated: bred by humans to eliminate undesirable characteristics and improve desirable ones.

edible: safe to eat.

enormous: very large; huge.

esophagus: the tube inside the body that passes food from the throat to the stomach.

extend: to spread or stretch out.

femur: the thighbone, which connects the hind lower leg to the hip.

fetus: an unborn young still growing inside its mother.

habitat: the natural home of a plant or animal.

herbivores: animals that eat plants as their main food.

humerus: the bone that connects the shoulder to the lower part of the forelimb or arm.

impressive: able to cause a strong emotional response.

incisors: teeth at the front of an animal's mouth used for cutting; elephant incisors are tusks.

inhabit: to live in or on.

jungle: tangled brushy growth.

larva: the wingless, wormlike form of a newly-hatched insect; in the life cycle of insects, amphibians, fish, and some other organisms, the stage that comes after the egg but before full development.

lobe: a curved or rounded part that sticks out.

mammals: warm-blooded animals with backbones that produce milk to feed their young.

mate (v): to join together (animals) to produce young.

matriarch: a female, usually a mother, who rules a family, group, or herd.

monotremes: a group of lower mammals including the platypus

(Australia) and the spiny anteaters (Australia and New Guinea). They do not give birth to living young, but lay eggs.

offspring: the young of a person, animal, or plant.

oviparous: able to produce eggs that develop and hatch outside of the mother's body.

ovoviviparous: able to produce eggs that develop inside the mother's body, which hatch there or just after being laid.

ovum: a small egg in an early stage of growth.

placenta: an organ inside the mother's uterus through which nutrition and waste pass to and from the developing baby.

poacher: a person who kills or takes game or fish illegally.

pregnancy: the state of carrying developing young inside the mother's body.

prehistoric: something that lived or happened before people began to keep written records.

prey (v): to hunt and kill another animal, usually for food.

prominent: standing out, or projecting beyond a surface.

Quaternary: the geological period from 2.5 million years ago up to the present; it includes the Ice Ages, the evolution of humans, and the extinction of a great many species of mammals.

savanna: a flat, grassy plain with some scattered trees.

scapula: the shoulder blade.

species: animals or plants that are closely related and often similar in behavior and appearance. Members of the same species can breed together.

spermatozoid: the male reproductive cell; sperm.

suckle: to nurse; to draw milk from the mother's body.

survivors: animals, plants, or humans that continue to live.

symbiosis: the living together of two unlike organisms, usually for the benefit of both.

tapirs: mammals related to the horse and rhinoceros. They are 6 - 8 feet long (1.8 - 2.4 m), stand about 40 inches (1 m) at the shoulder, and can weigh over 600 pounds (270 kilograms). They have heavy bodies with short, thick legs and a tapering face ending in a small movable trunk. Tapirs live in Southeast Asia and Latin America.

tibia: the bone that connects the femur to the foot.

trachea: the main breathing tube that carries air into the lungs.

tuck: to pull in or draw up; to put away a loose end.

tusk: a long, pointed tooth that sticks out of the mouth.

ulna: one of two bones of the lower arm or forelimb; the other bone is the radius.

umbilical cord: the internal cord that connects a fetus to its mother's placenta.

uterus: the part inside a mother's body where the young develop until birth.

viviparous: able to produce living young from inside the body.

ACTIVITIES

◆ Family life is important to elephants and helps each group survive. Some other mammals have also developed a family life-style, such as the wolf, the gorilla, and the whale. Choose an animal with a family life and make lists from library books of how its way of living is similar to or different from the elephant's family life. How does this style of living help your chosen animal survive in the wild?

◆ Visit a zoo, and compare Asian and African elephants. List the differences between the two types, such as the outlines of the ears or the shape of the head. Make a rough sketch of each comparison in your notes. Be sure to label to which kind of elephant each sketch belongs.

◆ Plastics have largely replaced elephant ivory, but the ivory is still being used to make decorative items. Elephants, slaughtered for their tusks, are nearing extinction. What can humans do to help elephants survive? What should be done with tusks recovered from poachers?

MORE BOOKS TO READ

African Elephants: Giants of the Land. Dorothy H. Patent (Holiday)
Animal World: Elephants. Jane Goodall (Simon & Schuster Children's)
Elephant. Sarah Blakeman (Troll Communications)
The Elephant. Christine Denis-Huot and Michel Denis-Huot
    (Charlesbridge)
The Elephant in the Bush. Ian Redmond (Gareth Stevens)
Elephants. Annette Barkhausen and Franz Geiser (Gareth Stevens)
Elephants: Our Last Land Giants. Dianne M. MacMillan (Lerner)
Endangered Mammals! ENDANGERED! series. B. Burton (Gareth Stevens)
In the Village of the Elephants. Jeremy Schmidt (Walker and Co.)
Mammoth. The Extinct Species Collection. H. Amery (Gareth Stevens)
One More Elephant: The Fight to Save Wildlife in Uganda. Richard Sobol
    (Dutton Children's Books)

VIDEOS

Elephant. (Encyclopædia Britannica Educational Corporation)
Elephant Diary. (Direct Cinema, Ltd.)
Elephants. (Rainbow Educational Media)
Elephants in the Wild. (GoodTimes Home Video Corporation)

PLACES TO VISIT

Adelaide Zoo
Frome Road, Adelaide
SA, Australia 5000

Granby Zoo
347 Bourget Street
Granby, Quebec J2G 1E8

Denver Zoo
City Park, 2300 Steele St.
Denver, CO 80205

Valley Zoo
Buena Vista Road and
    133rd Street
Edmonton, Alberta
T5R 5R1

Auckland Zoo
Motions Road
Western Springs
Auckland 2
New Zealand

National Zoological Park
3000 Connecticut Ave. NW
Washington, D.C. 20008

Mugga Lane Zoo
RMB 5, Mugga Lane,
Red Hill
Canberra, ACT
Australia 2609

INDEX

Answers to ELEPHANT SECRETS questions:
1. **b**
2. **c**
3. **b**
4. **b**
5. **a**
6. **c**